The Boy Named Boy

Ernesto Cuevas

The Boy Named Boy
© 2025 Ernesto Cuevas

This is a work of nonfiction. Names, events, and places are used truthfully based on the author's memory, experiences, and available documentation. Where necessary, certain details have been modified, condensed, or changed—including the names and identifying information of select individuals—to protect privacy or improve narrative clarity. While every effort has been made to preserve factual accuracy, this memoir reflects the author's perspective and lived experience.

For information regarding permissions, licensing, or special requests, please contact: author.ernestocuevas@gmail.com

First Edition, Paperback

ISBN: 978-1-968098-10-0

Printed in the United States of America

Dedication

For **Patricia**,
who stood by me when the ground gave way.

And for my children—
Joshua, Cody, Brandie, Ziarah, and Axel—
who gave me reasons to keep fighting,
even when the battles were silent and unseen.

This is for you—
for your loyalty, your love, and your
unbreakable belief in me.

You are the truest part of my story.

Prologue:
The Cry in the House

I was found crying in a house no one lived in.

I don't remember the wallpaper, or whether there was any at all. I don't remember the broken windows, the creaking floor, the smell of dust and rot. But I've imagined it so many times, I might as well have lived it.

They say someone heard me from the sidewalk. A stranger, walking past. Maybe on their way to work, maybe just out for air. They heard a noise—faint at first, like a cat, or a pipe knocking through the walls of an empty place.

But it wasn't a cat. It was me.

The Cry in the House

A newborn baby, crying in an abandoned house.

No note. No blanket. No explanation. No mother's scent lingering on my skin.

The police came. Then Catholic Charities. I was wrapped up, carried out. No one knew where I came from. No one knew my name. For weeks—maybe months—I was just *the boy in the house*.

That's what they called me.

And then came Tino and Frances.

They were already in the process of adopting two other children. Catholic Charities called them, said, "There's another child. A boy. Would you be willing to take him too?"

And just like that, I became part of a family. Their family.

The Boy Named Boy

They gave me a name—Ernesto Cuevas—and a home. Clothes, photos, trips to the beach. But no one ever told me how it began. That part of the story was tucked into a drawer and sealed shut.

I didn't find out until decades later.

One day, one of my aunts—my adoptive mom's sister-in-law—sat me down and said, "Did they ever tell you the truth?" Her voice trembled. Then she told me everything: the house, the crying, the stranger who found me.

She cried as she spoke, like it had haunted her for years.

And then, years after that, another aunt—one who lived in a different state and didn't even know the first one—told me the same exact story.

The Cry in the House

They couldn't have rehearsed it. They hadn't even met each other.

That's how I knew it was real.

The story I'd been living all my life had been missing its first chapter. And suddenly, I had it.

That's the thing about being adopted. It's not always the event that shapes you—it's the silence around it. It's the pictures where you look like no one else. The whispered comments from strangers. The ache in your chest you can't explain.

My birth certificate didn't even list a name. Just one word: *Boy.*

Boy Cuevas.

Like I was a placeholder. A question that hadn't been answered yet.

The Boy Named Boy

But this is my story. The story of a boy found in a house, and everything it took to become a man who knows who he is.

And I'm telling it now—for the boy I used to be, and for anyone else still searching the silence.

Chapter One: The Boy Who Didn't Belong

I didn't find out right away.

For most of my life, I thought my story began the way everyone else's did—parents, home, baby pictures in a frame. I knew I didn't look exactly like the rest of my family. I knew I didn't quite match. Blonde hair in a sea of black. Pale skin in a brown-skinned household. But no one ever talked about it. Not directly.

I was raised by Tino and Frances Cuevas. They loved me. They clothed me. They taught me how to ride a bike and how to bait a hook. And there was a whole family around them—grandparents, aunts, uncles— mostly on my dad's side. His father, Matias, and his mother, Christina, lived in Alamo,

Texas. Strong people. Traditional. They called me *mijo*. Gave me sweets. Hugged me hard.

My mom's parents—Pancho and Petra—were in Edinburgh, just a short drive from the border. Every summer, we made the long trip south to see them. Twenty-four hours in a station wagon, stopping at rest areas, watching my dad cook breakfast on a camp stove while my mom poured us juice from a cooler. Those memories are stitched into me, sweet and warm.

There was love in that family. Real love. But there was also distance—something beneath the surface I couldn't name. Even my grandparents looked at me a little differently sometimes, like they weren't quite sure whose face they were looking into.

Still, I didn't question it—not openly. I was a kid. You accept what you're given. You live the story you're handed.

The Boy Who Didn't Belong

It wasn't until years later—decades, really—that the truth broke the surface.

One day, one of my aunts—my adoptive mom's sister-in-law—sat me down and asked, "Did your parents ever tell you how they found you?"

I blinked. I had no idea what she meant.

She hesitated, then told me: "You were found, Ernie. Alone. In an abandoned house."

I didn't know what to say. My mind went blank and loud at the same time. She cried as she spoke, guilt welling up behind her eyes. "Maybe I shouldn't have said anything," she whispered. "But I thought you should know."

That story could've ended there—one person's account, maybe dismissed.

But then, another aunt—years later, from another state, someone who didn't even speak to the first—told me the same thing. Same story. Same words.

And that's how I knew it was true.

My life hadn't started the way I thought. It hadn't started with a nursery or a warm embrace.

It started in a cold, empty house.

With a cry.

I've tried for years to picture the house.

I don't know where it was exactly. I've never seen a photo. But I've built it in my mind, from scraps and shadows, like piecing together the ruins of a dream. In my mind, it's always the same: two stories, windows with missing panes, the front door cracked open like a mouth frozen mid-scream. A place not meant for living. A place meant for forgetting.

And inside that place was me.

The Boy Who Didn't Belong

No one knows how long I was there. Maybe a few hours. Maybe longer. Long enough to cry myself hoarse. Long enough for someone walking by to stop and wonder, *What is that sound?*

That stranger—whoever they were— heard me. They must've paused, looked at the house, maybe thought *no one lives there.* But the crying didn't stop. And something in them said, *check.* So they stepped inside. And they found me.

A baby.

Alone.

No bottle. No blanket. No note. Just a pair of small lungs doing the only thing they knew how—screaming into the dark.

That's the first image of my life: not a mother's arms, not a gentle voice, but a wail echoing through a dead house.

The Boy Named Boy

There's a part of me that still lives in that silence. That still feels the walls closing in. That still wonders who put me there—and why they walked away.

I was just a baby, so I don't remember it. But it lives in me anyway, like a scar beneath the skin. It's strange, how you can miss something you never had. A voice saying your name. A face leaning over your crib. A promise whispered in your ear: *You are wanted.*

I never got that.

Instead, I was picked up by police. Or maybe by an ambulance. Or maybe by a social worker with gloves and a clipboard. I'll never know the details. Those records are buried, if they exist at all.

All I know is this: I was delivered not by birth, but by accident. Handed not to a mother, but to a system.

The Boy Who Didn't Belong

And when Catholic Charities called
Tino and Frances and said, *There's a boy here.
Do you want him too?*, they said yes.

And that's how my life began.

With a yes from strangers.

With a cry in an empty house.

Tino and Frances had already made up
their minds.

They were adopting two children—
Alfredo and Dolores. A brother and sister, full-
blooded, dark-haired, solemn-eyed. They had
gone through the paperwork, the interviews, the
prayers. Their decision was sealed. Two
children. A pair. That was the plan.

Then the call came.

Catholic Charities told them there was
one more child—a boy, found alone. No
background. No known relatives. Just a baby.

The Boy Named Boy

They asked, *Would you take him too?*

It wasn't supposed to be three. That wasn't the plan. But something in them said yes.

Maybe it was faith. Maybe it was guilt. Maybe it was something unspoken—something that said this boy wasn't just extra. He was supposed to be there.

And so I was brought home.

Not chosen from a list. Not matched by a caseworker. Just handed over. One more life to fold into the Cuevas household.

I wonder sometimes what that day was like for them. Did they hold me awkwardly, unsure how to bond with a baby that wasn't theirs? Did they whisper promises to love me? Did they see me as a blessing—or a burden?

I'll never know.

The Boy Who Didn't Belong

What I do know is that from that day forward, I was raised as a Cuevas. My last name was given to me. My new identity printed neatly on paper. A name, a home, a beginning.

But beginnings don't erase what came before. They just bury it.

And buried beneath my new life was a silent fact: I was added last. Unexpected. Extra.

The "bonus child."

Tino was a government worker, Frances a stay-at-home mom at the time. They lived in a modest home in Mitchell, Illinois—a small town where everyone knew everyone. Their roots ran back to Texas, but they'd settled in the Midwest, raising a family of three that looked, from the outside, like any other.

But inside that home, secrets were kept. Questions were quietly answered with smiles and distractions. I wasn't supposed to know. None of us were.

We were told to keep it quiet. Even after we found out, years later—we were told *Don't tell anyone you're adopted.*

As if it were something to be ashamed of.

But even as a child, I knew. I could feel it in the spaces where love didn't quite reach. In the way my mother looked at me when she was angry. In the names people whispered when they thought I couldn't hear.

That one—he doesn't look like the others.

They were right.

I didn't know I was adopted—not back then. I was just a kid, running barefoot across the hardwood floor, chasing shadows, chasing my siblings, thinking the world was exactly what it looked like.

But something always felt... off.

My brother and sister—Alfredo and Dolores—had dark brown eyes and curly hair. Skin the color of sun-warmed earth. They looked like our parents. I didn't.

My hair was pale. My skin almost white. Even my eyes didn't match. In family photos, I looked like the neighbor's kid who wandered into the frame.

Relatives had a name for me—*Güedo.* "White boy." They said it with affection, but it stuck like a burr. At school, people whispered. "You sure you're from the same family?" "You don't look Mexican." "You must be adopted or something."

That last one stung. I didn't even know what adoption meant. But I knew it wasn't supposed to be said out loud.

I carried that quiet question for years.

There's this photo I remember—burned into my brain like the negative of a memory.

It's a studio portrait. We're all dressed up, lined in perfect rows: my dad in the back, proud and broad-shouldered; my mom beside him, hair carefully done; then us kids, sitting in front—Alfredo on the left, Dolores in the middle, and me on the right.

They looked like they came from the same sun. I looked like I came from the reflection of it.

Alfredo's hair was jet black, shiny and curly. Dolores's also had curls, soft and full. And then there was me—blonde. Pale. Like the light had passed through me instead of settling in.

At that age—five, maybe six—I didn't think about genetics or bloodlines. I just thought, *Why don't I look like them?* Why do people stare when we're in public? Why do the ladies at the store whisper when my mom pushes me in the cart?

I remember sitting in that cart once, my legs dangling, and hearing it:

"That boy doesn't look like the others."

I didn't understand what it meant at the time, not really. But my mother's silence afterward told me everything. She didn't correct them. She didn't say, *Of course he's mine.* She just pushed the cart faster, like distance could erase the question.

But deep down, a seed was planted. One that would take years to grow roots.

The Boy Named Boy

I didn't have the words for it then. I just knew I didn't fit. Not completely. Not in the mirror. Not in the eyes of strangers.

And certainly not in that portrait.

No one ever said the word.

Not back then. Not when it might've helped make sense of everything. My parents smiled through it. Dodged the questions. Redirected the conversations. And we—my siblings and I—learned not to ask.

But I felt it.

I felt it in the way my mom—Frances—sometimes looked at me. Like she was trying to see someone else in my face and couldn't find who she expected. Like I was a mistake she never said out loud.

There was love in our house, but it didn't always reach me.

The Boy Who Didn't Belong

When my brother messed up, it was a warning. When I messed up, it was a condemnation. The tone changed. The patience disappeared. The words cut deeper.

And sometimes, they weren't even about what I'd done—they were about *who I was*.

I remember one day, after a small argument over nothing—just kid stuff—she looked at me with that tight, quiet anger and said, *"I wish I never got you."*

I was maybe seven or eight. Old enough to understand. Old enough to pretend I didn't.

And then there was the time I told her about what happened—when that older boy touched me inappropriately during a family visit. I built up the courage. I was shaking. I was vulnerable.

And she laughed.

Laughed.

Said something like, *"Oh, it didn't hurt you."* Like my pain was a punchline. Like the silence she had lived with all her life was now mine to inherit.

That moment didn't just hurt—it confirmed something I had already begun to suspect: that my place in this family wasn't built on the same foundation as theirs.

I didn't know I was adopted. Not yet. But I knew I was different. I knew that sometimes, love has borders. And I was always skirting the edge.

We didn't talk about feelings. We didn't talk about origins. We didn't talk about anything that mattered.

We smiled in pictures. We ate together at dinner. We said prayers before bed. But there were walls inside our house that no one ever touched.

And I was behind one of them.

Our house wasn't cold or cruel all the time. My dad, Florentino Cuevas—Tino—was a good man. He didn't say much, but he didn't have to. He worked hard. Came home tired. Sat quietly in his chair most evenings unless he had his guitar.

When he played music, something in him softened. I'd sit nearby and listen, watching his fingers move like they were telling their own story. He didn't say "I love you," but I felt it more from him than anyone else in that house.

Frances, my mom, was the opposite. Loud. Sharp. Everything came out with an edge.

She wasn't affectionate—not really. She never hugged us just because. She didn't sit with us, or listen, or ask how we felt. But she *did* say she loved us.

Always out loud. Always when someone else was there to hear it.

I used to wonder who she was talking to. Sometimes when she said it, I'd turn my head like I misheard. *"Are you talking to me?"*

That's what it felt like—a line she said for the sake of appearances. Like a script she pulled out when someone else was in the room.

Behind closed doors, the words disappeared.
Behind closed doors, the volume went up.

I remember one day, Alfredo did something small—maybe knocked over a game or laughed at the wrong time. Frances picked up a checkerboard and brought it down on the top of his head. *Hard.*

Blood ran down his scalp.

Tino had to grab her. He pulled her back, held her by the arms and shouted:

"¡Lo vas a matar!" You're gonna kill him.

He said it in a voice I didn't hear often—scared, angry, urgent. The kind of voice that stays with you.

And I stayed with that voice. With the silence. With the feeling that even when we were together, we were never quite safe.

I didn't know I was adopted. Not yet. But I knew I was different. I knew that sometimes, love has borders. And I was always skirting the edge.

The answers would come. Not all at once. Not kindly. But the silence was cracking.

Soon, I'd learn why.

Chapter Two:
Mike at the Door

It started like any other day. I don't remember what we were doing — probably watching TV or getting ready for dinner. The sun was still out. I remember the light coming through the front windows, soft and low.

Then there was a knock.

I went to the door, and everything changed.

A man stood there—stocky, sharp-faced, wearing a military-style haircut and the kind of serious expression you don't forget. He looked like he'd been traveling. Dust clung to his boots. His shoulders were tight with purpose, like he'd been carrying something a long time and was finally ready to put it down.

He didn't fidget. He didn't ask for anyone by name. He didn't glance around like a stranger unsure of his welcome.

He looked straight at Frances.

And she—my mother, always sharp, always composed—didn't flinch.

She didn't ask who he was. Didn't act surprised.
She just said, "Mike."

Her voice didn't crack, didn't soften.
She didn't move for a hug. She just stood there like a statue remembering how to breathe.

I froze behind the hallway wall, peeking around the corner.

It was the first time I'd ever seen her like that—not angry, not sweet, just… still.

Mike at the Door

Like she'd been bracing for this moment for years. And now here it was.

She stepped aside and let him in.

Mike walked slowly into the living room. He scanned the space like it meant something to him. Then his eyes landed on Alfredo, and I saw his whole face shift—just a little. Not with shock, but with recognition.

It was like finding your reflection in a place you didn't expect.

I looked at them both. And in that moment, I saw it too.

They could've been twins.
Same jaw. Same dark brown eyes. Same skin tone. Same posture. They both carried themselves like they were used to disappointment—like they expected people to leave.

Frances sat down. Tino stood behind her, arms crossed, watching.

No one told us kids to leave the room. And I was glad. I didn't want to miss this.

Mike looked at Alfredo. Then Dolores. And finally said, "I'm your brother."

Just like that. No warning. No soft landing.

A truth dropped in the middle of our living room like a stone through glass.

And somehow, I knew this wasn't just their story.
It was mine too.

The living room got quiet after that.

The kind of quiet that isn't peace. The kind that hums in your chest like a warning.

We were adopted. That was the truth. But it wasn't offered like a fact to understand—

it was handed down like a sentence we were meant to serve silently.

The moment Frances said, *"Don't tell anyone,"* everything shifted.

Truth became burden. Relief became confusion. Something that could've opened a door just locked it tighter.

But I was too young to carry secrets well.

I told people. At school, in passing. Not proudly, not defiantly—just plainly, like someone finally had a name for the feeling they'd been walking around with their whole life.
"I'm adopted."

I thought it explained everything—and it did, in some ways. But it also brought trouble.

The Boy Named Boy

When Frances found out, she snapped.
Angry, disappointed. She made it clear: this
was not something we talked about. Not with
outsiders. Not with anyone.

"People will judge you," she said.
"They won't see you the same."

But they already didn't.

I knew that. I'd lived it. The stares. The
questions. The comments whispered just loud
enough to hear. "That one doesn't look like the
others." "You sure he's theirs?"

I had lived my whole childhood
standing beside a mystery.

Now that I had a word for it, they told
me to shut it down.

But the word was already growing
inside me.
Adopted.

Mike at the Door

It didn't make me ashamed—not yet. But it
made me curious.

If Alfredo and Dolores came from such
a painful place, and their story had seventeen
siblings and scars to prove it—what about me?

Who had I come from?

And why didn't they come looking?

Mike stayed.

Not just for a coffee or a quick
conversation—he stayed for days. Maybe a
week. Long enough for his presence to settle in
the air, long enough for the furniture to shift
around him like he belonged there. He wasn't
loud. He wasn't pushy. But he was constant.

And the whole house felt different.

Tino barely spoke while Mike was
there. He watched him from a distance,

cautious but not hostile, like a man trying to read a book he hadn't realized was written about him.

Frances moved through the house more briskly. Her voice sharper. Her shoulders tighter. The kind of tension that comes not from conflict, but from the weight of withheld truths.

And us kids? We followed Mike around like shadows.

He told stories—not dramatic ones, just bits and pieces. Life on base. Running drills. How he'd gone AWOL not out of fear, but to find his brothers and sisters. He had already located a few.

Then he said something that hit even harder:

"There are seventeen of us."

Seventeen siblings.

Mike at the Door

Each taken from the same home. Each
separated, split across different families,
scattered like leaves in a storm.

That's how bad it was.

Later, when my parents spoke quietly—
maybe thinking I wasn't listening—I heard
more.

Alfredo had cigarette burns on his back
and the soles of his feet when Tino and Frances
got him.

Dolores couldn't even sit up on her own
until she was two years old. Malnourished.
Underdeveloped.

They said Alfredo was protective of her
from the moment they came together. A little
boy, barely more than a toddler himself,
already stepping into the role of shield.

It must've been horrific. Bad enough for the state to not just remove the children—but to dismantle the entire family. Permanently. No reunification plan. Just separation.

Years later, after the truth of their adoption came out, Tino and Frances offered Alfredo and Dolores a choice.

"Do you want to meet your biological parents?"

They both said no.

Even after Mike's visit. Even after hearing about the seventeen siblings.

They didn't want to go back.

And that choice said everything.

Mike left the same way he came—in silence.

No dramatic goodbye. No packed-up ceremony. One morning, he just wasn't there.

Mike at the Door

His duffel bag was gone from the corner. His boots were no longer beside the door. The air felt lighter, but not in a good way. It felt like something had been taken out of the house, and something else had been left behind in its place.

Questions.

After he left, it was as if he'd never been there. Frances didn't talk about him. Tino acted like the visit had been a detour, not a detonation. But we knew better.

The house was quieter now, like everyone was listening to their own thoughts. Like we were each sitting in a different room, wondering what had just happened.

That was when Tino and Frances started making calls.

Not for me—for Alfredo and Dolores. They contacted Catholic Charities, looked into old records. Tried to piece together a trail.

Before long, we were on the road—
packed into the car, headed to Ohio. Then Texas.
Then back again. Visiting aunts, cousins,
siblings who had once shared a childhood with
Alfredo and Dolores. Strangers who looked at
them and saw their own eyes reflected back.

And me?

I went along for the ride.

I shook hands. Ate meals. Slept in guest
rooms.

But I wasn't a reunion.

I wasn't part of any tree they were trying
to replant. I was just *there*—a branch no one
could place. A kid who didn't look like anyone.
Who didn't belong to anyone in those houses.

No one said it out loud, but I felt it.

I was in the photographs, but not in the
bloodline.

Still, the people were kind. They hugged me, called me "mijo," welcomed me like I was part of something. But I could tell—they didn't see themselves in me the way they saw themselves in Alfredo and Dolores.

And the more doors we opened, the more I started to wonder if mine even existed.

Where were my people?

Where were the faces that would mirror mine?

Chapter Three:
Hurt in the Shadows

The drive was long.

I don't remember the name of the town.
Just that it was quiet, with cracked sidewalks
and weathered houses that leaned a little in the
wind. We had packed into the car again—Tino
at the wheel, Frances beside him, the three of
us in the back. These trips were becoming
familiar. Visits to people who weren't mine,
but who claimed my siblings like puzzle pieces
finally found.

This time, we were staying in a house
that belonged to one of Alfredo and Dolores's
older brothers. I don't remember his name.
Maybe I never knew it. Or maybe my mind

filed it away in a place where it didn't have to be touched again.

He was older than us—maybe late teens or early twenties. Quiet. He smiled when we arrived. Seemed friendly enough. He shook hands with Tino and Frances, gave Dolores a side-hug, clapped Alfredo on the back.

Me? He barely looked at me.

Which was normal. I wasn't the reason we were there.

That's how these trips always felt—like I was tagging along in someone else's reunion. I wasn't blood. I wasn't a missing piece. I was just… present.

They welcomed us into the living room. Offered drinks. Showed us where we'd be sleeping. Laughed about how the kids had grown. I sat on the edge of the couch and smiled when I was supposed to.

The Boy Named Boy

The house had that lived-in smell. Carpet that held on to years of cooking and cigarette smoke. Pictures on the walls—faces that meant nothing to me. Eyes that looked like Alfredo's. Like Dolores's. Not mine.

Night came fast. The grownups stayed up talking in the kitchen. I sat in the living room watching shadows stretch across the carpet. The brother—our host—walked in and looked at me.

"You can sleep in my room," he said. "I got space."

I hesitated.

Frances nodded from the kitchen. "Go on, mijo."

So I did.

Hurt in the Shadows

The room was dark. Just a little moonlight coming through the window blinds, slanting across the bed.

I sat on the edge for a minute, not sure where to put myself. He pulled back the covers, slid in without a word. I followed, keeping to the far side, careful not to let our arms touch.

It was quiet. No sounds except the distant murmur of voices from the kitchen, muffled by walls and time.

Then I felt it.

His hand.

At first I thought it was an accident. Just shifting under the blanket. But then it moved again—deliberate. Slow. It slid across my waist. Downward.

And then it was inside my pajama pants.

The Boy Named Boy

I froze.

The world narrowed to a pinpoint. My lungs stopped working. My limbs turned to stone. I didn't know what was happening, not really—but I knew it wasn't right. I knew it in my skin. In the way every part of me screamed *move* while my body couldn't obey.

My heart beat like a drum in my ears.

He didn't say a word.

I stayed like that—rigid, breathless—for maybe five seconds. Maybe less. But it felt like a lifetime.

Then I bolted.

I threw off the blanket, launched myself out of bed, and ran down the hallway barefoot, heart pounding so loud it drowned out everything else.

I didn't stop until I got to my parents' room.

I didn't speak. I didn't cry. I just climbed into bed next to them and pulled the covers over my head.

Frances shifted, maybe murmured something. Tino grunted in his sleep. No one asked me why I was there. No one pulled me close. No one noticed the way I shook.

And I didn't tell.

Not then. Not for years.

Because I didn't know how.

I buried it.

Not because someone told me to. Not because I wanted to forget.

I buried it because I had nowhere to put it.

I didn't know what had happened—not exactly. I didn't have the vocabulary. All I had was a feeling in my chest like a bruise that didn't show up on the skin.

I didn't tell my parents. I didn't tell my brother or sister. I didn't whisper it into a pillow or cry it into the night. I just... carried it. Quietly. Like a stone I couldn't name.

Life went on.

Trips. School. Church. Photos with forced smiles. That house faded behind me like a place I'd never return to—but the memory stayed.

It lived under the surface of everything. And I didn't touch it.

Not until years later.

I was grown by then. Grown enough to speak. To finally say the words out loud to someone I thought might care.

I told Frances.

I expected confusion. Maybe horror. Maybe softness. Maybe, for once, for her to look at me and really see me.

What I got was a laugh.

"It didn't hurt you," she said.

And just like that, it was buried all over again—this time under something worse: the realization that I wasn't worth believing.

I wasn't seen as a child who could be hurt. I was seen as a problem that didn't need solving.

That laugh has stayed with me longer than the touch ever did.

Because one was a moment.

The Boy Named Boy

The other was a verdict.

I don't remember the man's name. The one who touched me.

But I do remember the rage that built up inside of me whenever I recalled that incident. The feeling of wanting to murder that bastard.

I don't know whom I was more enraged at – that guy or my mother.

She was supposed to be the one who saw me. Who shielded me from the world and helped carry the weight I didn't ask to bear. But when I came to her with one of the deepest wounds of my life, she brushed it off like I was imagining it.

Like I was soft.

Like I was weak.

Like what happened didn't *matter*.

And that? That's what stayed.

Hurt in the Shadows

Her laughter wasn't loud—it was casual. Offhanded. Like I had just told her a weird dream, or a memory that didn't count.

"It didn't hurt you."

How could she know?

How could she even say that?

She wasn't in that room. She didn't see the way I ran, the way I shook, the way I couldn't sleep right for weeks. She didn't know that for years afterward, I couldn't let anyone sit too close behind me. Couldn't share a bed. Couldn't be in a dark room without a quickening heart.

But she didn't ask.

She didn't want to know.

I've thought about that moment more than I ever thought I would. Not because I needed her pity. But because I needed *her to care*.

To look at me and say, *You didn't deserve that.*

But she never did.

And maybe, deep down, that was when something inside me broke for good. Not because I was hurt—but because I was alone in it.

I've tried to forget that night.

I've tried to file it away in the drawer of things that happened a long time ago—before I had language, before I had armor, before I even knew who I was.

But it doesn't go away.

It shows up in the pauses between conversations. In the way I still flinch when someone enters a room too quietly. In the trust

I have to build from scratch, over and over again, with every new face in my life.

That night never ended.

It just went quiet.

And maybe that's the hardest part of carrying something like this—it doesn't scream. It whispers. It gets into the cracks of your life and waits for you to notice.

There are still days I wonder what might've happened if I hadn't run. If I hadn't said yes. If I hadn't been *there at all*—in a house I didn't belong to, surrounded by people who weren't mine.

I was a guest in someone else's reunion. I had no blood in the walls. No history in the pictures. But I'm the one who came back damaged.

And no one noticed.

No one except me.

But maybe now, that's enough.

Maybe telling it here—finally—is how the echo starts to fade.

Chapter Four:
Echoes of the Past

I started school in Mitchell, Illinois— Mitchell Elementary, just across the river from St. Louis.

I was five.

The first day should've been exciting. New shoes. Crayons with perfect tips. That tight little backpack that made you feel important. But all I remember is looking around and knowing instantly that I didn't quite fit.

The kids had dark hair, dark eyes. Some looked like my siblings. None looked like me.

I took a seat near the front of the room. My name was called. The teacher smiled. But I saw the moment—just a flicker—where her eyes paused on me a little longer than the others. Like she was trying to work out the math.

Later that day, someone asked me if I was in the right class.

Then another kid leaned over at lunch and asked, "Are you adopted?"

I didn't know how to answer.

At the time, I hadn't been told yet—not officially. But something in me had already guessed. And the question landed like confirmation. Even if I didn't say yes, they already thought I was.

I kept my head down. Ate my sandwich. Laughed when they laughed. But inside, a small, heavy silence settled in.

No one else got asked that. No one else had to justify their presence.

Just me.

That day marked something. A before and after. Before school, I was just a kid. After school, I was a question mark.

It didn't stop after the first week. Or the first month.

Teachers, parents at pickup, even the cafeteria lady—every now and then, someone would hesitate before calling me by my last name. Like they weren't sure if I was in the right family.

And I wasn't sure either.

It started at home.

Güedo.

That was the name my extended family in Texas gave me. Slang for "white boy." At

first, I thought it was just a nickname.
Everyone had one. Alfredo was "Beto."
Dolores was "Chelita." I was "Güedo."

But over time, it started to feel like
something else.

Not a name.

A reminder.

That I didn't look like the rest of them.

That I didn't match.

My cousins in South Texas said it with
a laugh, sure, but there was always a glance
that came after. A look that said, *He's not one
of us—not really.*

And it wasn't just family. At school, it
got worse.

Kids pointed. Whispered. Asked if I
was a visitor. A foster kid. A neighbor.

Even when they didn't say anything, I could feel their eyes on me when Frances came to pick us up. Her hair pinned up, dark skin in the sun, speaking Spanish to another parent in the parking lot. Me, standing beside her, pale as winter.

We didn't belong in the same silhouette.

Strangers thought I was the neighbor's kid. Some assumed I was adopted before I even knew I was. That was the hardest part—how they could see it before I did.

Racism wasn't some abstract thing. It wasn't just stories in history books. It was on the playground.

They called us "dirty Mexicans." Said things like, "Go back where you came from," even though where we came from was the same town they did.

Sometimes they used the N-word. They didn't care about accuracy. They just wanted to sting.

Even though I was light-skinned, I still got pulled into the slurs. I was guilty by association.

But inside our home, the echoes were different.

Frances didn't talk about race. She didn't talk about identity. She didn't say much unless it was with volume. But when people asked her about me—why I looked so different—she'd get stiff. Defensive.

"Of course he's ours," she'd say. But her tone was always edged. Always rehearsed.

Like she knew they were right to ask.

I didn't start out looking for fights.

They found me.

A comment here. A shove there.
Someone laughing too loud after calling me a
name I didn't understand until much later.

At first, I tried to ignore it. Walk away.
Keep my head down like Frances told me.
"Don't give them a reason."

But after a while, I didn't need a reason.

I needed respect.

And in that school, in that
neighborhood, you didn't earn it with words.

So I swung.

I swung because I was tired of the
whispers. Tired of being the one who always
had to explain himself. Tired of teachers who
called on me slower, like they weren't sure I
belonged. Tired of being asked if Frances was
my *real* mom.

The Boy Named Boy

By the time I was in third grade, I had a reputation. I wasn't the biggest, but I was fast. I didn't talk tough—I just didn't back down.

I fought kids who used slurs. Kids who said my siblings weren't really my siblings. Kids who said I was just lucky someone picked me.

Each time, I walked away with more than bruises. I walked away with space. With silence. With kids thinking twice before they asked me that question again.

Are you adopted?

No one asked after that.

It became part of my identity. The tough one. The one who didn't take anything. The one who hit first if you hit too hard with your words.

Alfredo didn't fight like I did. He was fast—he'd run when things got tense. Dolores? She could hold her own, especially with her mouth. She didn't swing, but she cut deep.

Me? I fought because it was the only language that seemed to work.

And maybe, deep down, I fought because I knew there was no one else coming to do it for me.

Even when I wasn't fighting, I was looking.

In the hallways. At the park. In the grocery store checkout line.

I looked at people's faces the way most kids looked at the toy aisle—hoping, maybe this time, I'd see something familiar. A jawline. Eyes shaped like mine. Ears that stuck out the same way.

Something to make the world make sense.

But I never did.

Everywhere I went, I was the kid who didn't match.

I looked at my reflection and saw a stranger. Not because I hated myself—but because no one else seemed to *claim* me. Alfredo had Dolores. Dolores had Alfredo. They even had Mike now—proof of where they came from.

Me?

I was the blank space in a family tree.

Even in church, surrounded by other Mexican families, I felt like a ghost sitting in someone else's pew. The other boys looked like their dads. The girls looked like their moms. The elders looked at me and smiled politely, but I saw it in their eyes:

Whose kid is that?

I smiled back. But inside, I kept searching.

Sometimes, I'd catch my own reflection in a window or a mirror and stop, hoping I'd see something new. Something that would tell me where I came from.

But the face looking back at me never answered.

Somewhere along the line, being tough became more than survival.

It became who I was.

The kid who didn't flinch. Who didn't cry. Who didn't care what people said— because I had fists, and I knew how to use them.

The Boy Named Boy

I leaned into it. Wore it like armor. Walked taller. Laughed louder. Built a wall around myself that felt safer than any hug I wasn't sure would come.

I became *the mask.*

The one people respected. The one even teachers started treating differently—like they didn't want to be on the wrong side of me.

But no one asked why.

No one asked what made a kid like me need armor that early.

They didn't see the questions I still carried. The ache in my chest when I saw fathers and sons who looked alike. The stillness inside me when someone said, "You've got your mother's eyes," and I realized no one would ever say that to me.

I got good at hiding it.

So good, I almost believed it myself.

But deep down, I was still that kid in the family photo—the one who didn't match. The one the birth certificate called "Boy." The one who learned to punch before he learned where he came from.

And no matter how many fights I won, I couldn't hit my way into belonging.

Chapter Five:
Building and Breaking

Patricia came into my life like a song I already knew the words to.

There wasn't a dramatic moment or a spark that lit the sky—it was quieter than that. Familiar. Natural. Like finding a place to rest after walking too far. We were young—too young to know what forever meant, but old enough to want it.

We met, we talked, we laughed. And then we didn't stop.

It didn't take long before we were serious. Serious in the way only teenagers can be—fast, intense, no brakes. We weren't thinking about tomorrow. We were thinking about *now*. How it felt to be wanted. To be seen.

Then she got pregnant.

We were barely out of school. Still figuring out who we were. But life didn't wait.

When she told me, I didn't panic. I didn't run. I didn't even flinch.

I just said, "Okay."

Because somewhere deep in me, I knew what it felt like to be left behind. To be unwanted. And I wasn't going to do that to someone else. Especially not my own child.

That child was Joshua.

When he was born, the world rearranged itself.

I remember holding him—small, warm, eyes barely open—and thinking, *I'm responsible for this now*. Not just his diapers or his food or his safety. But his heart. His future. His story.

And the truth is, I was still just a boy myself. I didn't have answers. I didn't even have my own beginning figured out. But I had love. And I had grit. And sometimes, that's enough to start with.

Patricia and I stayed together. Not because we had to. But because we wanted to.

She became my partner—not just in raising a child, but in building a life. Through the chaos. Through the pressure. Through the moments where it felt like everything could fall apart.

That was the start of our family.

Not perfect. Not planned.

But real.

And I knew, if I was going to build something that could last, I had to become more than what I was.

So, I made a decision.

I joined the Army.

I didn't join the Army because I loved war stories.

I joined because I needed a path—and fast.

Joshua had just been born. I had a girlfriend-turned-partner who was counting on me. And I had no college plans, no savings, no map. What I had was grit, a body that could take a hit, and a will to keep going when things got hard.

So, I walked into a recruiter's office.

The man behind the desk didn't have to sell me on it. I already knew. I wasn't there to browse. I was there to enlist. I told him I wanted something physical, something that paid steady, something that gave me a direction.

He signed me up.

A few weeks later, I was at Fort Benning, Georgia—boots on gravel, hair shaved down to regulation, voice hoarse from barking responses I barely understood yet.

Basic training was no joke. But something about it made sense to me.

The yelling? I'd heard worse.
The running? I'd been chasing something my whole life.
The discipline? That was just another kind of silence.

I learned fast.

Building and Breaking

Follow orders. Speak only when spoken to. Push through pain.

I had already done all of that—just in different ways, with different people.

And when it came time for Jump School, I didn't flinch. Strapping into a parachute and stepping into the sky felt no scarier than standing in front of a classroom that thought you didn't belong. I'd been jumping into the unknown my whole life. This time, at least, someone had packed the chute.

When training was done, they shipped me out to Fort Irwin, California—the National Training Center.

That's where I joined the OPFOR unit. Opposition Force.

Our job was to pretend to be the enemy—to dress in Russian gear, run drills, and be unbeatable. We were the test every soldier had to pass, and we were trained not to let them.

It was strange at first. Wearing the other team's uniform. Speaking in phrases that weren't ours.

But after a while, it started to feel normal.

Maybe because I was used to feeling like the outsider. Like I was always playing a role that didn't quite match who I was underneath.

But this time, I was good at it.

And people noticed.

At Fort Irwin, I started to feel something I hadn't felt in a long time—respect.

Not the kind you have to fight for on a playground. Not the kind you fake through toughness or silence. Real respect. Earned in sweat, precision, and grit.

Our unit was small, but tight. We trained hard, we trained smart, and we learned to move like one body. When you're part of the Opposition Force, your job is to be better than everyone else. Not just skilled—flawless. We simulated the enemy, and we were supposed to win. Every time.

And we usually did.

We didn't just wear uniforms—we wore each other's burdens. We knew who could run the fastest, shoot the cleanest, stay calm under pressure. We knew who had nightmares and who needed to be left alone after a long mission. It was a brotherhood, even if no one called it that out loud.

The Boy Named Boy

That silence—the one that haunted my childhood—started to make sense in the military.

There were no long talks about feelings. No explaining who you were or why you looked different. No teachers raising an eyebrow at your last name.

Here, it was simple:

Could you do the job?

If the answer was yes, you belonged.

And I did.

Then came Berlin.

That city carried history in its bones. Tension in the air. You didn't walk anywhere without checking your surroundings. You didn't assume anything was just routine.

There, we did more than just drills. We trained for real-world scenarios: hostage rescues, hijackings, counter-terrorism sweeps. Most of it happened at Tempelhof Airport—a Cold War relic turned urban training ground. We'd sweep rooms, run timed entries, practice precision maneuvers with live rounds echoing through hollow hangars.

One of the wildest parts was the people you'd run into. On paper, they were "support staff." But in the field, I started to recognize them for what they really were—Delta Force.

They moved differently. Watched everything. Didn't talk unless they had to. Some were guys I had known casually—until I put the pieces together. One glance, one nod, and I could tell. And judging by the look they gave me back, I had *blown their cover* without even trying.

But there was no tension—just respect. Unspoken. Heavy.

The Boy Named Boy

We were all there to do our jobs. Some in daylight. Some in the dark.

And for the first time in my life, I wasn't the outsider. I was part of something elite. Something focused. Something that made me feel necessary.

Even with all the chaos behind me—and more ahead—this was the closest I'd ever felt to belonging.

But even as I built a name for myself in the field, even as I felt stronger and more certain than ever, there was still something under the surface. Something restless. A tension in my chest I couldn't quite place.

I was doing everything right.

But there was still a part of me that didn't feel whole.

Building and Breaking

That feeling followed me all the way to Berlin.

Berlin felt like the edge of something.

It was the late 1980s. Cold War tensions were thick, but most people didn't feel it— unless you were stationed on the line. Unless you were close enough to the Wall to feel its shadow stretch into your sleep.

I was deployed there after California. New orders. New climate. New terrain. But the work? The pressure? That was the same.

Except now, it wasn't just drills.

One night, I was supposed to meet up with Sergeant Kenneth Ford—a buddy from another battalion. We'd been planning to catch a drink and maybe blow off steam at a club downtown: La Belle Discotheque.

The Boy Named Boy

It was late. Midnight, maybe later. I arrived just as he hit the dance floor—music blasting, lights spinning, everyone moving like the world outside didn't exist.

I stood by the entrance, watching him. Thought about waving. Decided to wait until he came off the floor.

Then everything exploded.

A roar, louder than anything I'd ever heard. The walls cracked. Glass rained down. The floor beneath the dance floor gave way, swallowing people in an instant.

One moment, Kenneth was dancing. The next, he was gone.

There was screaming. Smoke. Flames. Sirens trying to cut through chaos.

And I moved.

Building and Breaking

I don't remember deciding to—I just did.

I ran inside, coughing, eyes burning. Pulled people out. One after another. I remember grabbing a woman whose legs were torn open from debris. I remember dragging a man whose shirt had melted into his skin.

I couldn't see much. The smoke turned everything black. My ears were ringing. My chest hurt.

At some point, something hit me—a shoe, maybe a chair, something hard—and I went down. Blood ran down my face. I couldn't tell if it was mine.

But I kept going.

I must've pulled five or six people out before I collapsed on the sidewalk, coughing so hard I thought my lungs would rip.

The Boy Named Boy

They said it was a bombing, later. That it had something to do with Libya. That it was part of something bigger. Political.

But all I knew was that my friend died on that dance floor.

And a part of me did too.

They patched me up after Berlin.

Stitches. Bandages. Time.

But the headaches never stopped.

I don't know if it was the blast or the weight of what I saw that night, but something stayed behind in me. A pressure. A buzzing. Like part of me never left the smoke.

I didn't talk about it much. Nobody did. In the Army, you move forward. That's what we were trained for—keep walking, keep serving, keep quiet.

But the noise didn't stay quiet inside
me.

I had dreams. Smell of burning. Sound
of screaming. The floor giving out.

I'd wake up in my bunk sweating. My
fists clenched. My chest tight. Sometimes I
didn't even remember the dream—just the
feeling it left behind.

Still, I didn't stop.

A few months before I left Berlin, they
offered me a new job.

"You want to drive for the G3?" they
asked.

The second in command of the Berlin
Brigade.

I still had six months left in my
enlistment. I didn't hesitate.

The Boy Named Boy

I got handed the keys to a bulletproof Mercedes and spent my days driving a full-bird colonel across the city—to meetings, security briefings, diplomatic visits. My uniform was pressed, my boots polished, and for the first time, I felt like I wasn't just another body in the machine—I was trusted. Visible. Chosen.

It was a good gig. The calm before civilian life. My last assignment before I had to figure out who I was without orders. Without missions.

But Berlin was still Berlin.

There were ghosts in that city. And every so often, one of them came into view.

From time to time, I'd get pulled for guard duty at Spandau Prison.

Only one man was locked up there by then.

Building and Breaking

Rudolf Hess.

Hitler's former deputy. One of the architects of the Nazi regime. A man who had flown to Scotland in 1941 on some strange peace mission, been captured, tried at Nuremberg, and sentenced to life in prison. Now, decades later, he was still there—the last prisoner in a fortress built for hundreds.

I remember standing outside his cell, listening to the silence.

It didn't feel like I was guarding a man. It felt like I was guarding a ghost.

He was frail. Old. A shell of whatever monster he might've once been.

But even then, the air around him felt heavy—like history hadn't quite finished speaking.

The Boy Named Boy

It was strange, standing there. Thinking how close I was to someone who'd once stood beside Hitler... and how far I'd come from the boy they called "Boy" on a torn birth certificate.

That's Berlin for you.

You go in thinking you're just another soldier.

And you walk out knowing you've brushed up against the weight of the world.

When the time came to hang up the uniform, I did.

But a part of me stayed in Berlin.

Buried in the smoke.

After Berlin, I kept serving. Got reassigned. Stayed in shape. Pushed through. Because that's what I knew how to do—build forward. Lay bricks on top of pain and call it a foundation.

I had a wife back home. A son who needed me. A name that carried weight in my unit. I couldn't afford to break—not then.

But part of me already had.

The boy who had once sat at the edge of a family photo, unsure where he fit, had become a man standing at the edge of war, unsure who he was anymore.

The only thing I knew for sure?

I was still carrying something that hadn't found a place to land.

Chapter Six:
Blood and Betrayal

Berlin never felt safe—not really.

Even before the bombing, there was a tension in the air, like the city was holding its breath. Divided city. Divided people. It gets into your bones after a while. Makes you walk a little differently. Makes you watch doorways and windows without realizing it.

I was on duty again—post-bombing. The tension hadn't gone away. It just shifted. Thickened.

We got word: a soldier had gone rogue. Gone missing. They believed he was hiding out in a part of the city we weren't supposed to be near without backup.

Blood and Betrayal

The Stardust—a grimy building that
used to be a club, now half-abandoned and full
of shadows.

I was part of the team sent to sweep it.

I remember the plastic butcher curtains
hanging over the back exit—thick, clear strips
that clung to your clothes as you passed
through them. The smell of cigarettes and damp
concrete.

I walked through those curtains and the
world flipped.

Three of them.

The fight broke out fast—loud, messy,
hands flying before words could.

I didn't start it.

But I finished it.

They pulled knives.

The Boy Named Boy

I saw the glint before I felt the pain.

One blade drove into my back. Another into my side. Another behind my knee.

Seven wounds in total.

Seven lines of heat and shock carving themselves into my body.

But here's the thing no one expects:

You don't always fall down when you're stabbed.

I didn't.

I fought.

And when it was over, it wasn't me lying on the ground.

It was them.

I walked away.

Bleeding. Breathing hard. Alive.

Blood and Betrayal

I made it to the roadside and sat down, my body screaming at me to stay awake, stay alert.

Blood poured from the wounds—warm and fast.

I didn't have bandages.

I didn't have help.

So, I pulled off my socks and plugged the stab wounds myself.

Sat there, on the side of a Berlin street, cramming socks into deep, open cuts like it was the most normal thing in the world.

Not because it didn't hurt.

But because giving up wasn't an option.

By the time help came, I was still sitting there— stubborn, bleeding, breathing.

Alive.

And determined to stay that way.

They stitched me up. Gave me painkillers. Told me I was lucky.

But what they couldn't patch was the question:

Why do I keep surviving things I wasn't supposed to go through in the first place?

After I got stabbed in Berlin—seven times, fast, brutal, no warning—I spent three months in the hospital recovering. I remember lying there, hooked up to machines, drifting in and out, wondering how I hadn't died.

The wounds were deep. One of them— behind my knee—cut through tendons. It made even sitting feel like an insult.

When they finally let me go, I wasn't marching anywhere.

Blood and Betrayal

I walked with a cane for a while.
Dragged my leg through hallways, across
gravel yards, up metal steps.
Slow, stiff, stubborn.

But I didn't quit.
I didn't take a medical discharge.
I didn't let the wounds decide who I was.

I finished my service.

They gave me a new assignment—
lighter duty.
Nothing too physical. Nothing that would tear
open what was barely holding together.

Still, I showed up every day.

Still, I wore the uniform.

Still, I held my head up when others
looked away.

It wasn't easy.

The Boy Named Boy

I had to teach my body to trust itself
again—
To walk.
To run.
To climb.

Little by little, I pushed.

I made it back onto my feet without the
cane.

And when my time came, I left the
Army on my own terms—not because they sent
me home, but because I finished what I started.

Some people get medals.

Some get ceremonies.

Me?

I got my life back.

And for a man like me, that was worth
more than any ribbon they could pin on my
chest.

I had been stabbed seven times in the line of duty. My lungs still burned when I walked fast. My back ached when it rained. I got migraines that felt like knives behind my eyes.

But I embraced it all. I had found something that made me feel part of something larger. Something that didn't ask where I came from. It only asked if I could perform. And I did.

And now, it was gone.

Just like that.

I was a civilian again.

Back to Illinois. Back to family. Back to a version of me I wasn't sure still existed. A man who had seen people die, who had pulled bodies from fires, who had stared into the eyes of men trying to kill him—and now had to figure out how to make small talk at dinner.

The Boy Named Boy

The medals didn't matter at home.

The scars didn't earn you space at the table.

I didn't come home to a parade.

I came home to silence.

And that silence was louder than any battlefield.

I went back to Patricia.

To our small house. Our son. Our life.

The world didn't stop just because I had nearly died. The mail still came. Bills still needed paying. My son still needed to be fed, played with, held. Patricia still needed a partner—not a ghost walking around in a soldier's skin.

And that's what I was, at first—a little ghostly.

Blood and Betrayal

I couldn't sleep the same. Couldn't go into crowded rooms without checking exits. My back ached constantly. The headaches came in waves that knocked me flat. And every once in a while, I'd catch a sound—an engine backfiring, a chair scraping—and I'd be back in Berlin. Back under smoke. Back in the fire.

But I never said any of that out loud.

Because what could I say?

"I think I left part of myself in a building that's no longer standing?"

"I think I'm scared of peace?"

Instead, I tried to do what I'd always done—keep moving forward.

I worked odd jobs when I could. Helped around the house. Smiled at cookouts. Hugged Joshua tighter than he probably understood.

The Boy Named Boy

I tried to focus on building a future,
even as the past still clung to my boots.

I called my parents every day.

Checked in.

Told them about the little wins, the
tough days, the strange new silence of civilian
life.

They were happy to hear from me—
always warm on the phone.

But the kids I grew up with?

Dolores and Alfredo?

Nothing.

No calls. No letters. No "How are you
doing?" Not even a holiday card.

It hurt more than I expected.

Because we'd grown up through the
same fire, held the same secrets—and

somehow, when the smoke cleared, they didn't
seem to notice I was missing.

Or maybe they did, and just didn't care.

My parents, though—Frances and
Tino—they tried.

They'd drive all the way from Texas to
Illinois just to visit me, just to make sure I
didn't feel abandoned.

At first, I thought it was kindness.

Later, I realized it was guilt.

See, while I was gone—working,
bleeding, rebuilding—
Tino was handing out money like candy.

$2,000 here.
$3,500 there.
Sometimes up to $5,000 a week to my adoptive
siblings.

The Boy Named Boy

Funding their lifestyles while I was scraping by, trying to put my body and mind back together.

When I found out, I didn't let it slide.

I called it out.

Told them flat out how absurd it was— how backwards it felt that the kid who never asked for anything was being left behind while the ones who took and took kept getting rewarded.

And you know what?

Frances and Tino agreed with me.

They knew it wasn't right.

They said the words.

But they didn't draw the line.

Sometimes love looks like sacrifice.

Other times, it looks like refusing to see the truth when it's standing in front of you.

And no matter how many miles they drove to see me—

There were miles between us they never knew how to cross.

Sometimes, the bravest thing you can do is stop chasing the people who never turned around.

In the quiet that followed—after the distance, the letting go—I found my way back to something that never betrayed me.

Music.

My guitar playing took off in a way it never had before. Like every scar had tuned the strings tighter. Like the part of me that had been shot at, stabbed, ignored, and silenced had finally found its voice.

I started writing. Not just songs—whole albums.

Once, I wrote a full set of music and lyrics in five days for a friend, Col. Perry Sullivan, a retired Air Force pilot who was writing a book about his father—Lost Flowers, the story of moonshine runs and foxhound hunts in the Carolina woods.

I gave the project everything I had. Because in the music, I wasn't just telling *his* story—I was telling mine too.

Chapter Seven:
Fire and Flight

Not every war happens on a battlefield.

Some happen on backroads, in deserts, in the still moments after you've come home but haven't settled in.

These stories—these wild, twisted, *did-that-really-happen?* kind of stories—don't fit cleanly into boxes. They're not in the files. They're not in the medals. They don't come up in job interviews or family dinners.

But they're part of who I am.

After the Army, life didn't slow down. It got weirder. Louder. Sometimes more dangerous.

The Boy Named Boy

People think once the uniform comes off, the adrenaline stops. The chaos fades. But for me, it was just a new kind of mission—stay alive, stay sane, and maybe, laugh a little along the way.

So here's what I remember.

Not because I planned to.

Because I survived it.

It was supposed to be a hunting trip.

Me and Max Rahn, my buddy from Fort Irwin, had planned it like a military op—gear packed, weapons checked, route memorized. We were after chukars, those fat, fast little birds that lived deep in the Mojave. Like quail, but meaner.

We left late—real late. Wanted to be two hours into the desert by the time the sun started to rise.

Fire and Flight

It was dark. Cold. Quiet.

We were a long way from pavement when we saw the tire tracks.

That was the first red flag. Out there, that far from anything, you don't see signs of life unless someone's got a reason to hide. And these tracks were fresh. We followed them.

Eventually, the trail led to an old, beat-up hippie van, parked next to some massive desert boulders.

Then we heard it.

A woman's voice.

"Help."

Faint. Ragged. Just one word, but it hit like a slap.

We stopped about forty yards out. Got out. Stood real still.

Then the van's door opened.

And a very tall man stepped out—completely naked. No clothes. Just a high-powered rifle in his hands. Like something out of a nightmare.

He didn't say a word. He just raised the gun and started shooting.

Max dove behind the driver's door. I hit the dirt. Bullets tore through the air, ripping into the truck, shattering the windshield, blowing out windows like soda cans. We were outgunned and out-positioned.

Max fired back with his pistol. Then he tossed me the shotgun.

It was loaded with birdshot—not ideal against a man with a sniper rifle, but it was what we had.

Fire and Flight

I popped up, aimed for the flash, and pulled the trigger.

Hit him. Saw him stagger. Red mist across his chest and arms. He didn't go down, but he paused. Long enough for Max to jump in the truck.

"Get in!" he yelled.

I dove through the passenger door. He grabbed the wheel, I stomped the gas.

We tore out of there, both of us laying flat on the seat, bullets whizzing overhead, glass still falling from the ceiling. One shot pierced my coat sleeve, missing my shoulder by inches.

We drove two hours through the desert, wounded, shaken, and furious. Made it to Victorville, found the nearest law enforcement outpost, and filed a report.

The Boy Named Boy

Later, they told us what we'd interrupted.

The man was raping the woman in the van when we arrived.

We didn't save her because we were heroes.

We saved her because we were hunting chukars and made the wrong turn at the right time.

Max was pissed—his truck had just gotten a new paint job that day. The windows were gone. The body was shot full of holes.

But we were alive.

And the man?

"Full of birdshot," they said.

That was enough for me.

Fire and Flight

It was close to the Fourth of July, the desert was dry, and I was feeling restless.

So I did what I always did when the world got quiet—I stirred it up.

Me, my wife, and Evette Hoy—another soldier's wife—piled into our Chevy Chevette and headed out into the Mojave. Just a casual drive into nowhere. The girls were very pregnant, bellies round and full of new life, but that didn't slow us down.

I had a little *party kit* with me. Nothing crazy. Just a few artillery simulators, some flash grenades, and—okay—one live grenade.

We were miles from anything when we saw it.

A bonfire, burning big in the distance, way off the road.

The Boy Named Boy

Dozens of kids out there—locals, probably. Drinking, lighting fireworks, playing music. Looked like a scene out of a beer commercial. I figured they wouldn't mind a little extra excitement.

So I asked, *"You guys want to see something cool?"*

They said yes.

I tossed the first artillery simulator. Boom. They jumped. Laughed.

Then the flash grenade—a blinding white pulse. Now they were nervous.

And then I pulled out the real one.

Pulled the pin. Lobbed it right at the edge of the bonfire.

It landed.
It ticked.
It blew the whole damn fire to hell.

Fire and Flight

Logs scattered. Sparks lit up the sky. Kids screamed and ran like a bomb had gone off—because one had.

I turned back to my car, cool as hell, and said, "Alright, let's go."

We were laughing. My wife was half-worried, half-cracking up. Evette kept saying, "Ernesto, what the hell did you just do?"

We were a few hundred feet from the highway when it happened.

Two big SUVs—maybe Suburbans—pulled across the road and blocked us in.

Men got out.

They weren't in uniforms, but they weren't just partygoers either.

"You guys know anything about explosions in the desert tonight?"

The Boy Named Boy

I handed my wife my six-pack of beer and whispered, *"Hide this under your dress."*

She did.

I looked at the guys and shrugged.

"That party was out of control, man. We were just trying to leave."

They looked us over. Looked at the women. Looked at the dust on the Chevette.

And let us go.

I hit the main road, turned off the lights, and floored it.

By the time we got home, I slid the car under the awning, turned off the ignition—and that's when I heard it.

Chop-chop-chop.

A helicopter. Big one. Searchlight scanning the neighborhood.

Fire and Flight

It hovered above us for a minute,
spotlight bouncing off our roof.

Then it moved on.

We sat there, hearts pounding, windows
down, beer under my wife's dress.

I called that a close call.

Others might've called it something
else.

Me? I just called it a good story.

Through all the madness—bullets,
bombs, close calls—I always came back to one
thing.

Music.

It was the first language I understood
before the world got complicated.

When I was a kid, I played drums—beat
rhythms into plastic chairs, tabletops, anything

that echoed. In school, I picked up the saxophone. Played in bands, marched in parades. It was structure and chaos at the same time. Just like me.

And when I came back from Berlin—stitches healing, nerves raw—my guitar became the thing that made sense.

I didn't read music. Didn't need to.

I felt it.

Each chord was a memory. Each lyric was something I hadn't said out loud.

Some guys drown their trauma in a bottle. I poured mine into strings.

After the service, I started writing. A little at first. Then more. Before I knew it, I had a stack of songs and a sound that was completely mine—gritty, honest, full of soul and sand.

Fire and Flight

One day, I got a call from a buddy—
Col. Perry Sullivan, ex-Air Force. Said he was
writing a book about his father, Percy Flowers,
a legendary moonshine runner and foxhound
hunter from North Carolina.

He asked if I could write some music to
go with it.

I said, "Give me five days."

And I did it.

An entire album. Lyrics. Guitar. The
whole story wrapped in melody.

Because music was never just a hobby.

It was how I survived.

Out in the swamps, on the ranges, in
dusty fields and training bases, I met musicians
from every corner of the country. We'd pull out
guitars by firelight. Share verses. Trade stories.
Play until the mosquitoes stopped caring.

That was church.

That was therapy.

And it always reminded me of Tino, my dad. The way he played guitar at home—quiet, never flashy, but full of soul.

That part of him lived in me.

No matter what I'd lost—family, friends, connection—music was mine.

Still is.

People ask how I made it through the things I've seen. The war. The street. The desert. The home I came from.

I tell them the truth:

Instinct.

Some folks are born lucky. Some are born brilliant.

Fire and Flight

Me? I was born watching. Listening. Reading people, terrain, silence.

Whether I was in a foxhole, driving a colonel through Berlin, staring down a naked man with a rifle, or hiding from helicopters with a beer under my wife's belly—I trusted my gut.

It never lied.

And when it did whisper, I listened.

There were nights where a second's hesitation would've left me bleeding in the sand. Moments where someone else might've froze—but I moved. I ran. I drove. I fired back.

It wasn't fear. It wasn't bravery.

It was something deeper.

The kind of instinct you only earn when you grow up unwanted, then spend your life earning your right to exist.

The Boy Named Boy

The world looked at me like I was supposed to disappear.

I didn't.

Instead, I played music in its face. I laughed in deserts. I wrote songs on pain. I survived things that should've killed me—and I did it without losing my fire.

I wasn't lucky.

I was ready.

Always.

Chapter Eight:
Uncovering the Name

I never expected answers.

Not really.

When you grow up adopted and nobody talks about it—*really* talks about it—you start to believe the silence is permanent. That it's not just a lack of information, but a wall that was built on purpose.

But after the Army, after the music, after the chaos of those wild post-service years, something shifted.

Maybe it was age. Maybe it was fatherhood. Maybe it was just time.

I wanted to know.

Not just what happened. Not just the where or the when. I wanted to know who I was before they gave me a name.

So I started digging.

Not with drama. Quietly. On my own time.

I reached out to Catholic Charities—the same organization that placed me with Frances and Tino.

At first, it was like pulling teeth. Records sealed. Files misplaced. People "weren't authorized." I kept calling anyway.

Then I called hospitals. County offices. Vital records departments. Any place that might hold a slip of paper with something— *anything*—on it.

Uncovering the Name

I wasn't chasing a fantasy. I didn't expect a tearful reunion or a long-lost mother to come running out of the mist.

I just wanted truth.

Even if it hurt.

Even if it was incomplete.

Because the silence I'd grown up with wasn't neutral—it had weight. It had pressure. And I was tired of carrying it.

So I kept going.

One phone call at a time.

One form at a time.

Until pieces started to surface.

The first real breakthrough came like most truths do—small, plain, and undeniable.

I learned I had been found.

The Boy Named Boy

Not at a hospital. Not in a clinic. Not even left in the care of strangers.

I was discovered in an abandoned house.

Some man—a stranger—found me there. I don't know why he was there or how he heard me. Maybe I was crying. Maybe I was just lucky.

He called the police.

They came. Took me into custody. No parents in sight. No one to claim me. No name on file.

Just a baby.

Three or four months old.

Malnourished. Weak. No birth certificate. No file number that led anywhere meaningful.

Uncovering the Name

They handed me over to Catholic Charities.

And that's where Frances and Tino came in.

They weren't looking for a baby—not exactly. But Catholic Charities contacted them and said, *"We have a child who needs a home."*

And they said yes.

They took me in.

They gave me a new name.

They raised me.

And for a long time, that was supposed to be the end of the story.

But years later—when I was grown, long out of the house—two different aunts told me the same thing:

"You were found in a house. All alone."

The Boy Named Boy

Neither of them knew each other well.
Neither had anything to gain from the story.
But they said it like it was common knowledge.
Like it had always been part of the family
folklore—just never told to me.

"You were abandoned."

They didn't say it to be cruel. They said
it like it was fact.

And in that moment, I realized it had to
be true.

Because if two people from different
sides of the same tangled tree knew the same
root...

Then that root was mine.

It arrived in the mail, tucked inside an
envelope that felt too thin to carry something so
heavy.

Uncovering the Name

The paper was old—thin, yellowed slightly at the edges, like it had been waiting a long time to be read.

I laid it out flat, smoothed the corners, and stared at it like it might speak.

But the first thing I saw wasn't a name.

It was a blank.

Right where a name should've been, where every birth certificate in every file cabinet across America said *John* or *Melissa* or *Daniel*, mine said:

Boy.

That was it.

No first name. No last.

No place of birth. No time stamp.

And the part that should've listed my mother?

Torn.

Not scratched out.

Not left empty.

Torn.

Like someone had physically ripped her name from the page. As if she could undo me just by erasing herself.

It didn't feel like paper anymore. It felt like a verdict.

I stood there a long time, holding the proof of something I had always felt but never seen:

That I had come into this world unclaimed.

Unrecorded.

Forgotten by whoever should've held me first.

Uncovering the Name

No blanket. No photo. No memory passed down through stories.

Just Boy.

The paperwork confirmed it all— everything I'd been told, and everything they hadn't.

I was abandoned.

Not metaphorically. Literally.

Found in a house. Crying. Alone. With no name to cry out.

There's something strange about seeing the truth in print.

It doesn't yell. It doesn't accuse. It just sits there, quiet. Permanent.

That birth certificate didn't give me closure.

It gave me clarity.

For years, I'd tried to fill in the blanks. I imagined where I came from, who my mother might've been, what my name was before they gave me a new one.

But the truth was colder—and cleaner.

I had no name.

I wasn't named and given away.

I was never named at all.

And somehow, that felt like the most honest thing I'd ever learned.

Because everything else in my life had always come with conditions. Love that had to be earned. Family that disappeared when it got hard. Smiles that disappeared behind closed doors.

But this?

This was fact.

Uncovering the Name

I wasn't claimed.

I wasn't remembered.

But I was here.

I had made it through warzones, bar fights, backwoods gunfire and silence at the dinner table. I had raised a family, buried friends, written songs that held pain no one else could carry for me.

And I had done it with a name that came not from a birth, but from persistence.

Ernesto Cuevas.

That wasn't the name I was born with.

Because I wasn't born with one.

It's the name I survived into.

And I'll carry it until the end.

Chapter Nine:
Found and Forgotten

It started with a TV show.

The Locator. One of those docuseries that helped people find long-lost relatives— mothers, fathers, siblings, even childhood friends lost to time. The kind of show where the big reveal always ended in hugs, tears, and a happy soundtrack.

I used to watch it late at night, wondering what it would be like to be the one found.

But that wasn't my story.

I wasn't the one people were looking for. I was the one who'd been left behind. Hidden.

Found and Forgotten

Still, the show got under my skin. It stirred something.

After it ended, I started searching. Quietly at first. I wasn't sure what I was hoping to find—just that the not knowing was starting to feel louder than anything else in my life.

I started with what I had: a few scraps of information, a torn birth certificate, and a vague memory that someone had once said my mother's last name might've been De Los Santos.

So I went online.

I found a small genealogy site that helped track family names—nothing fancy, but it was a start. I searched De Los Santos and found a handful of people who might've been related.

And then I sat down and wrote letters.

Not emails. Real letters. Page by page, asking one simple thing:

"Do you know of a woman from Ohio who may have had a child in 1963?"

Most people wrote back politely, saying no.

But some replies hinted at something more.

"We never heard anything about a baby…"
"She went away for a while, but no one ever said why…"
"If she was pregnant, she kept it a secret."

There were no confirmations. No confessions. Just shadows.

But shadows meant something had been there.

And now I needed more than speculation.

I needed answers.

By 2015, I'd hit a wall.

The letters helped. They opened doors. But they didn't give me what I needed. I still didn't have names. Faces. Connections I could stand in front of and say, *I came from here.*

So I found someone who could.

She was a private investigator out of Long Beach, California. Sharp. Professional. She didn't offer sympathy—just results.

"Five days," she said. "I'll find your family in five days."

She did it in three.

I scraped together the money—$1,500, which wasn't easy at the time. But this wasn't about affordability. This was about finally putting the questions to rest.

Her results came fast and loud:

"Your biological mother's last name is De Los Santos."

She confirmed the rumors, the letters, the loose ends I'd been following all along. Suddenly it was real. Tangible. And it didn't stop there.

She gave me names, addresses, locations. A list of people with blood ties— people who had walked the earth all these years, never knowing I existed.

And then—buried in that list—was something that made me sit back in my chair and stare:

She found a sister.

I had a sister.

The PI found her name. Her married surname. Her last known address. Even the name of her son—a man named Allen Reynolds.

For a moment, I just sat there.

Not because I didn't believe it.

Because I did.

Because part of me always knew there had to be someone else out there carrying the same missing pieces.

I didn't wait long.

Next, I went looking for Allen.

The investigator gave me a name: Allen Reynolds.

He was my sister's son. My nephew.

I didn't know what he looked like. I didn't know what kind of life he had. I didn't even know if he knew I existed. But I had a name, and sometimes that's all it takes.

I started asking around—quietly, carefully. I found someone in the area near Ashland, Ohio who said, *"I don't know Allen personally, but I think I know where he lives."*

He pointed me to a place nearby—a little country spot called the Olivesburg General Store.

So I did what anyone would do in the twenty-first century.

I Googled the store.

Sure enough, it had a presence. A Facebook page. A number.

I called.

A woman picked up—friendly, curious, and a little skeptical when I told her what I was doing. I explained who I was looking for. Why I was looking. She listened.

Then she said something I'll never forget:

"I think I know Allen Reynolds. We're Facebook friends."

I asked if she'd be willing to message him for me. Just to say I was looking. That I had a question. That maybe—just maybe—this wasn't a mistake.

She did.

And within the hour, my phone rang.

It was Allen.

He sounded surprised. Careful, but not afraid.

"Wait—you're who?"

I told him. Slowly. Everything I knew. The name. The search. The investigator. His mother—my sister.

There was a long pause. Then a kind of breath, like something unlocking in real time.

"No one ever told me I had an uncle."

We talked for a long time. Nothing heavy at first. Just the basics. Voices. Vibes. Feeling it out. He didn't shut down. He asked questions. He wanted to know more.

We kept in touch over the next few months.

Eventually, I met him in person.

And then—finally—I met his mother.

My sister.

The one who'd lived a whole life parallel to mine. A woman with my blood who had never known I was out there, breathing the same air.

After meeting Allen and my sister, the path opened wider.

I knew the name now—De Los Santos—and I had faces to go with it. But I wanted more. I wanted to look into the eyes of people who might remember something. Who might say, *"Yes. We knew."* Or maybe, *"We didn't—but we're glad you found us."*

The next connection came through a man named George De Los Santos—a cousin.

He didn't just reach out—he got on a plane and flew from Texas to Virginia to meet me face-to-face.

We sat down like we'd always known each other. There wasn't any awkwardness. No testing the waters. He looked at me and said,

"You've got our blood. I see it."

I believed him.

A few months later, I flew out to Laredo, Texas—George's home.

That's when the reunions really began.

I met cousins, aunts, even distant relatives who'd only heard of me through whispers. There was curiosity, yes. But not judgment. Not rejection.

They didn't ask me to explain myself. They asked where I'd been.

And then I met Irma.

My aunt. But not just any aunt— "The Tamale Queen" of Laredo. That's what everyone called her. She ran a business making tamales and had a presence that filled the room before she even spoke.

She hugged me like she meant it. Fed me like I was already hers.

There was no pretense. No caution. Just belonging.

At a family gathering, someone pointed across the yard and said,

"You see that guy? That's Gary De Los Santos."

I blinked. That Gary.

The Texas Ranger. The one I'd seen on TV for years—cases, interviews, news clips. He was a fixture in the state. Respected. Recognizable.

And now, he was standing twenty feet from me.

A man I'd watched from a distance was suddenly family.

The Boy Named Boy

It felt like a trick. Like the world had folded in on itself and finally made room for me.

Because for the first time, I wasn't standing on the outside looking in.

I was in the photo.

And no one asked me to leave.

I waited a long time before calling her.

Not out of fear. Out of caution.

I had found the family. The name. The sister. The nephew. The cousins. They all confirmed what I had spent a lifetime questioning.

But she—the woman who gave me life—was still a ghost.

And ghosts don't always want to be found.

Found and Forgotten

Her name came to me through the investigator. Her number, too. She was living a quiet life, far from where I'd been left. And I had every reason to believe she knew exactly who I was.

Still, I was careful when I called.

I introduced myself gently. Told her my name. Told her about Catholic Charities. The adoption. The torn birth certificate. The name no one gave me.

She listened.

And then she said,

"I don't know who you are."
"You've got the wrong person."
"I never had another child."

I didn't argue.

But I knew she was lying.

The Boy Named Boy

She tried shifting blame—said I might've belonged to her twin sister.

Said there must be some confusion.

But I'd already spoken to her son. To my sister. I'd met cousins, held family photos in my hands. The people who knew her best knew the truth.

And eventually, so did she.

Her husband—Larry—spoke up. Told her she should tell the truth.

There was a pause. Then, in the quietest voice I've ever heard someone use to describe their own child, she said:

"Yes. I had a baby. But I never named him."

That was it.

No apology. No questions. No *Why did you call me?* or *I've wondered about you all these years.*

Just that cold fact.

Like a name whispered into a canyon and never echoed back.

I hung up the phone.

There wasn't anything left to say.

She'd admitted it—but only after being cornered by facts. By names. By voices she couldn't deny anymore. And even then, she didn't ask about me. Didn't want to know who I'd become. Didn't say the words I think part of me had hoped for, even after everything.

There was no "I'm sorry."

No "I remember your face."

No "I wondered what happened to you."

The Boy Named Boy

And still, I wasn't angry.

I was tired.

Because I'd already survived it once.

Being abandoned as a baby is something you don't remember—but you carry it anyway. You carry it in the way you double-check people's love. In the way you stay quiet when you're hurt. In the way you look in the mirror and sometimes wonder, *Would someone have kept me if they'd known me?*

But being denied as a man?

That's different.

Because now I had a name. A life. A family of my own. I wasn't crying in a house anymore—I was standing on solid ground. And she still looked through me like I was a rumor.

Her brother, Carlos, a retired Army colonel, called me later.

He'd heard what happened.

"She's had a hard life," he said.
"Please… try to be kind to her."

And I wanted to say I understood.

But the truth is, I didn't need to be kind.

I needed to be done.

So I let her go.

No anger. No resentment. No
expectation that she'd ever find her way back
to me.

I had met her. Heard her voice. Given
her the chance.

She gave me birth—but she never gave
me anything else.

Not a name.

Not a goodbye.

Not even a moment.

And still…

I existed.

I always did.

Chapter Ten: The Other Half of the Story

I didn't grow up wondering about my father.

Not the one who raised me—Tino Cuevas—but the man whose blood had marked me from the beginning. For most of my life, he was a blank. A question no one asked. A shadow without a shape.

That changed one day at the grocery store.

My biological mother—after years of denial—finally gave me a name.

Larry Ewing.

That was him. My father.

The Boy Named Boy

The name hit hard, like a stone through glass. Not because it explained everything, but because it confirmed something I'd always carried deep down: *he had existed*. Someone had been there at the start, even if he didn't stay.

I didn't stop there.

I did what I always do when the world gets quiet—I investigated.

I took a DNA test. Not to prove her wrong, but to prove the truth to myself.

And it came back clear.

The name matched.

I connected with members of the Ewing family—his relatives. His sister, her son. They welcomed me with kindness. No judgment. Just openness.

Then came the deeper twist.

The Other Half of the Story

Larry had a brother.

Also now gone.

And when I met his brother's children—my cousins from Nebraska—they stared at me and said something that stopped me cold:

"You look just like our dad."

Not kind of. Not maybe.

Exactly.

It threw everything into a new light. The timing. The DNA. The face in the mirror.

Could Larry have been the wrong Ewing?

Even now, I don't know for sure.

All I know is that one of those brothers gave me life—and both of them are gone.

The Boy Named Boy

Larry, the man my mother named, was a Vietnam veteran.

He served in Vietnam. Came home. And took his own life.

That's what I knew at first.

But then my aunt—his sister—told me something I wasn't prepared for.

She said Larry didn't just struggle because of the war. He struggled long before it.

He grew up in a violent home.

Their father—my grandfather—was abusive.

Cruel without reason.

He would beat Larry for nothing. Make him stand still with beer cans on his head…
…and then shoot them off.

The Other Half of the Story

That's not discipline.

That's a man turning a child into a target.

She said Larry never really recovered. Not from the house. Not from the war.

It was like the damage started in his own home, then got sealed into his bones overseas.

By the time he came back from Vietnam, he was already carrying too much.

And eventually, it took him down.

I sat with that for a long time.

I'd been to war too. I knew that silence. That weight. That spiral that people don't talk about unless they've lived it.

It didn't make me pity him.

It made me understand him.

The Boy Named Boy

We were both sons of war. Both carrying things no one else could see.

He didn't make it.

I did.

But I've never stopped wondering what part of me came from him.

After I confirmed Larry Ewing as my biological father—or possibly his brother—the next door opened almost naturally.

I began reaching out to the Ewing side of the family.

It started with one name. Then another. Cousins. Aunts. People I never expected to find, much less hear on the other end of a phone line saying:

"We're glad you found us."

That alone meant more than I could say.

The Other Half of the Story

The most unexpected part?

The kindness.

There was no suspicion. No "Are you sure?" No emotional distance.

They knew Larry. They knew his brother. And when I sent photos, the response was instant.

"You look just like our dad."

That was from Larry's brother's children—my cousins in Nebraska.

I hadn't even told them what I'd been told. I let them look at me. And they saw it.

Same face. Same eyes. Same frame.

"It's like you stepped out of one of our old family photos."

They weren't trying to convince me of anything.

The Boy Named Boy

They were just acknowledging what they saw.

That kind of clarity—unprompted, pure—doesn't happen often in stories like mine.

We built something after that.

Not a full reunion. But connection.

We stay in touch. Share stories. Photos. Birthday messages. The kind of normal family stuff that, for me, feels anything but normal.

I haven't met them all in person yet. But I know their names now.

And more than that—I know where I come from.

Not just biologically.

Emotionally.

The Other Half of the Story

Because when someone looks at you
and says, *"You look just like someone I loved,"*
it doesn't matter how late you showed up in the
story.

You still belong in it.

The truth was already written on their
faces—but I needed something concrete.

So I took the DNA test.

Not for them.

For me.

For the boy listed as "Boy" on a birth
certificate with no name, no mother, no record
beyond survival.

The test confirmed what I already knew
in my bones:

I was family.

The Boy Named Boy

To the De Los Santos on my mother's side.

To the Ewings on my father's.

The connection was clear. No room for doubt.

And still, the story wasn't simple.

Because Larry had a brother, and that brother's children saw their father in me.

Same build.

Same smile.

Same stubborn jawline that doesn't flinch, even in hard light.

And though I never met either of those men, the resemblance told its own story—one written in bone and breath, not memory.

There's something eerie about looking at a photo of someone you never knew... and seeing your own face looking back.

The Other Half of the Story

That's what it was like.

No timeline could explain it better than that.

No test could outmatch the moment a cousin looked at me and said,

"You're ours. We've always known."

As for my siblings on my father's side—they know who I am.

I haven't spoken to them.

They haven't called.

No letters. No texts. Just mutual awareness, like names scratched into opposite sides of a door that neither of us has opened yet.

I've made peace with that.

They don't owe me anything.

But the door's still there.

The Boy Named Boy

Maybe one day it'll open.

Maybe it won't.

Either way, I'm not waiting.

Because the part of me that needed proof has it now—in DNA, in photographs, and in the way those cousins said my name like it had always been part of the family.

Later, when I visited Nebraska to meet Joe and the other cousins, he didn't just show me photos or tell stories.

He took me to the house where my biological father had lived.

Then he drove me out to a military cemetery—a small, quiet plot where Larry Ewing was buried beneath a clean white headstone.

That alone would've been enough.

But Joe wasn't done.

The Other Half of the Story

He brought me back to his house and handed me something I never expected to see.

The .22 revolver Larry had used to take his own life.

He placed it in my hand.

I stood there, in the presence of Larry's grave, holding the very weapon that ended his life.

And then I did something that may sound strange to anyone who hasn't lived through a story like mine:

I took pictures.

I stood over Larry's headstone, the revolver resting atop it, and took photos of me holding it—not for show, not out of disrespect, but because it was part of the truth.

The same way some people keep letters or fingerprints, I kept that image.

The Boy Named Boy

That was my biological father in the ground.

That was the gun he used.

And this—this was the end of a search that started before I had a name.

Joe still has the revolver. He said maybe one day he'd give it to me.

Maybe.

I don't know if I'd keep it.

But I'll never forget what it felt like— the weight of it, the history of it, the sorrow folded into steel.

Some stories are too strange to be fiction.

Like how the place my father Tino used to play music—Ramone's Restaurant—became the same place I'd one day walk into to meet Joanne, my cousin, for the very first time.

The Other Half of the Story

It wasn't planned that way.

I didn't even know it was the same place until I was already inside, waiting for her. I looked around, and it felt familiar. Not just from childhood memories—but something deeper, something already lived.

Joanne walked in, and I froze.

She looked familiar. Too familiar.

Not in a deja vu way.

In a *my-brain-has-seen-this-person-before* way.

We started talking. And everything clicked into place.

Joanne's mother—who worked at Ramone's for years—was my aunt.

But not just any aunt.

The Boy Named Boy

She was the identical twin sister of my biological mother.

Let that sit for a second.

Joanne's mom and my birth mom were twin sisters—and my adoptive parents, Frances and Tino, knew them.

They knew the restaurant owners.

They went to dances with them— Mexican community events, full of music and food and kids running around under the stars while grownups swayed to old love songs.

Frances. Tino. Joanne's mom. My mother.

All in the same room.

Over and over again.

My biological mother used to visit every year.

The Other Half of the Story

She'd stay with her sister—Joanne's mom.

They'd go to Ramone's. Go to the dances.

Be in the same places where I was.

And no one ever knew.

Not Joanne.

Not Frances or Tino.

Not even me.

But I remembered.

Not with facts.

With faces.

When I first saw a photo of my biological mother, I didn't ask "Who's that?"

I said, *"I've seen her before."*

Maybe not directly.

Maybe not up close.

But I recognized something. A movement. A look. A shared energy.

Same with Joanne.

When we met, I didn't feel like I was meeting a stranger.

I felt like I was finally seeing someone again.

My adoptive parents went to their graves never knowing.

Never realizing they'd spent years around the very family they thought they'd replaced.

And my biological mother?

She stood just a few feet away at those events—laughing, dancing, maybe even looking in my direction once or twice—without ever claiming me.

The Other Half of the Story

And I wonder sometimes if she felt anything.

If seeing me play among the other kids made her heart shift in her chest.

Or if denial is strong enough to erase even your own child's face.

What I know for certain is this:

My two families weren't strangers.

They were neighbors.

They were dancers in the same room.

And I was there—between them, unseen, unlabeled, unforgettable.

Chapter Eleven: The Farm and the Fire Inside

There's a spot in Michael, Illinois—a little town most people have never heard of—where two rivers almost touch. The Mississippi and the Illinois. And right between them, wrapped in woods and quiet, is where I live.

Not just where I sleep.

Where I live.

It's not a neighborhood. It's not a subdivision. You don't hear dogs barking next door or kids on bikes or garbage trucks early in the morning.

Out here, it's just me, my family, and the land.

The Farm and the Fire Inside

I own sixty acres of thick forest and open field. Long stretches of trail where I can ride my four-wheeler, work the soil, or just walk with a cup of coffee in hand and watch the mist roll through the trees.

There are days I don't see another soul besides my own.

And I like it that way.

After everything I've been through—the houses I was shuffled through as a kid, the Army barracks, the hospitals, the visits with people I thought might be family—this is the first place that's truly mine.

No uniforms. No silence. No guessing games.

Just animals, tools, sunrise, and work.

The kind of work that makes your hands tired and your mind still.

I've got horses, pigs, chickens, rabbits, turkeys. Some for food. Some just to take care of. Every day starts early and ends late. There's always something to fix or feed or clean or corral.

But I wouldn't trade it for anything.

There's a rhythm to it. A truth.

I know when it's going to rain just by the smell of the trees. I know the tracks of every animal that crosses my land. I know which fence line needs reinforcement, which tree is about to drop, which rooster's about to start trouble with the others.

It's not just farming.

It's learning to live on your own terms, after years of living on everyone else's.

No neighbors close enough to knock on my door. No traffic. Just space. Stillness. Time.

The Farm and the Fire Inside

And after all these years chasing identity, chasing answers, chasing family—

I found my peace right here, between two rivers and sixty acres of truth.

Every morning on the farm starts the same.

I roll out of bed before the sun's all the way up. I've got a routine—not because anyone tells me what to do anymore, but because out here, the land speaks in rhythm. If you listen close, it'll tell you what it needs.

And I listen.

I step outside and breathe in the air— thick with dew, earth, and woodsmoke from the night before. Sometimes there's fog rising off the treetops. Sometimes it's just a still, quiet sky waiting to warm up.

The animals are always up before I am.

The Boy Named Boy

The horses nudge their gates. The pigs grunt and shuffle, waiting for feed. The chickens are loud and dramatic, like they've got something to prove. The rabbits are quiet but always watching, like little spies in the corner of their pens. And the turkeys—well, they talk like they run the place.

It's a lot to manage, but it's good work.

Every pen has to be cleaned. Every trough filled. Every fence checked. I ride my four-wheeler out to the far corners of the property to make sure nothing's down—no trees blocking the trail, no gates left unlatched by wind or critters.

There's no one else out here to do it.

And that's the part I love most.

I used to live in chaos—other people's schedules, the military's orders, family members' silence, questions without answers.

The Farm and the Fire Inside

Now, I wake up and know exactly what my day will ask of me.

It'll ask for my time. My hands. My back. My patience.

And I give it.

Because every shovel of feed, every bale of hay, every patch of fence I mend—it adds up to something real.

Out here, I don't need anyone's approval. I don't have to wonder who I am. I don't have to explain myself.

I built this life.

With wood, sweat, and the need to finally be somewhere I could belong without question.

And when I sit on the porch at night, watching the sky go dark over trees that don't need anything from me, I don't think about the places I've been or the people who didn't stay.

I think about tomorrow's chores.

And how lucky I am to have them.

Raising kids changes the way you see the world.

And for someone like me—someone who was raised by people who could barely say "I love you" without an audience—it changes how you see yourself.

I didn't always know what kind of father I wanted to be. But I knew what I didn't want to be.

I didn't want to be the kind of parent who left scars in silence. Who loved only out loud when others were listening. Who couldn't say "I'm proud of you" without choking on the words.

The Farm and the Fire Inside

So I tried to show up differently.

Not perfect.

Just present.

I've got four kids of my own now. All grown, except for one. Each of them carrying their own piece of this story. Their own bloodline of strength and surprise.

Joshua—my oldest—is in construction. Solid kid. Independent. Works hard and lives with his girlfriend. He doesn't need much from me anymore, and that's how I know I did something right.

Cody, a year younger than Josh, is a carpenter. He builds offices and warehouses, the kind of work that makes him tired in a good way. We talk tools and trades now. It's funny how kids grow up and suddenly speak your language.

The Boy Named Boy

Brandie, my daughter, works for Jonah White, a neighbor and a good man. Jonah invented those Billy Bob Teeth and the hat with hair. Brandie helps out at his shop, working on the assembly line, keeping everything moving.

And then there's Ziarah.

My baby.

She was born in 2010, and she's still here with us, in the house, growing up on this farm the way I wish I could've grown up— surrounded by trees, truth, and people who see her.

She's smart. Quiet. Watchful. A lot like I was as a kid, but with something I didn't have back then: safety.

Last but not least, there's Axel—born in 2012. He's around a lot. Runs through the same fields, plays with the same animals, eats at the same table.

The Farm and the Fire Inside

There's something beautiful about that—watching generations stack up on land I built with my own hands.

When I found my biological family, the kids were shocked.

Not in a bad way—just surprised. Especially when I showed them pictures of my sister.

"She looks just like you," they said.

And she did.

That resemblance hit them in the gut the way it hit me.

It was like seeing a ghost with your own face.

But they were happy for me. Supportive. Curious.

The Boy Named Boy

They didn't grow up needing those answers the way I did—but they understood why I needed them.

And that's all I could ever ask for.

There's something about holding a weapon in your hands—not in war, not in fear, but in calm, in sport, in control.

For me, firearms were never about violence. They were about precision. Focus. That perfect moment between breath and trigger where the rest of the world fades out and it's just you, your skill, and the silence.

Back in the Army, I made my mark as a shooter. At one point, I set a live fire range record—the best they'd ever seen. Even the officers talked about it. And I carried that pride with me long after the uniform came off.

Out here on the land, I still shoot. Not for trophies. Not for attention.

The Farm and the Fire Inside

For rhythm. For clarity.

It's the same with fishing.

I've been dropping lines in water since I was a kid. I know the rivers, the lakes, the spots where the fish bite and the ones where they just wait you out.

There's nothing like it.

Standing waist-deep in water at dawn, watching the mist rise while the line sings through the air—that's church to me.

It's where I do some of my best thinking.

Where I remember who I've been… and who I don't want to be again.

I've got hunting stories too—some you've already heard, some I'll keep to myself.

The Boy Named Boy

Wild ones. Close calls. Moments that make you laugh and then stop laughing because you realize how lucky you were.

But more than the adrenaline, more than the skill, what I value most is this:

Freedom.

The freedom to walk my land with a rifle slung over my shoulder and no one to answer to.

The freedom to fish a quiet river with no clock ticking over my head.

The freedom to say, "This is mine," and not mean a gun or a catch, but a life.

After all the noise I grew up in—all the silence that followed—this is what peace looks like:

A gun cleaned and oiled, not pointed in fear.

The Farm and the Fire Inside

A rod cast into still water.

A man, finally still inside himself.

Chapter Twelve:
Music in My Blood

Before I could read.

Before I knew what adoption meant.

Before I had a name anyone spoke with softness—

I had music.

I was just a kid. A little boy growing up in a house where words were sharp, silence was common, and love came wrapped in discipline. But even back then, before I could understand my place in the world, I understood rhythm.

I had a drum set before I had answers.

And that drum set saved me.

Music in My Blood

It wasn't much—something pieced together secondhand. The kind of thing most parents would toss in a garage sale. But to me, it was everything.

I'd sit for hours, tapping out feelings I didn't have names for. Rage. Loneliness. Hope. Confusion.

Every beat was a question I wasn't allowed to ask.

As I got older, I moved to the saxophone.

In school, the sound of brass and breath became my sanctuary. The way it vibrated in my chest—the way it filled rooms—it made me feel bigger than I was. Like maybe I didn't need to shout to be heard. Like maybe the music could speak for me.

No one had to like it. No one had to clap.

The Boy Named Boy

It wasn't about applause.
It was about survival.

I wasn't the kind of kid who felt safe
asking for things. I didn't bring home problems
or open up to teachers or try to explain what
didn't make sense at home.

But give me an instrument, and I'd tell
you everything.

Not in words. In tone. In tempo.

Fast and sharp when I was angry. Slow
and searching when I was lost.

Even now, I think that's why music
stuck with me.

Because when everything else fell
apart—when people left, or lied, or looked
away—sound never did.

It stayed. It listened.

And in a world where I was never quite sure if I belonged…

Music always let me in.

When I got out of the Army, I didn't come back whole.

I came back stitched together—scarred in places no doctor could see.

My knee had been torn open. My back ached constantly. My head pounded more often than not. But that wasn't the worst of it.

The worst part was the quiet.

The kind of silence that lives in you, not around you.

No orders. No noise. No structure. Just a man left alone with everything he saw… and everything he still didn't understand.

That's when the guitar came back into my hands.

The Boy Named Boy

I'd messed around with it before. A few chords here and there. But now, it became something more.

Something necessary.

At first, it was just about keeping my hands busy—so I wouldn't drink too much or stare too long at nothing. But then it turned into something else. Something bigger.

The guitar started saying things I couldn't.

I'd sit for hours, strumming patterns that made no sense to anyone but me. Chords that hurt a little when I hit them just right. Strings that buzzed like ghosts at the back of my throat.

I wasn't just playing music.

I was exorcising something.

Music in My Blood

The more I played, the more I remembered who I was.

Not just the soldier.

Not just the forgotten kid.

But a man who could still create something beautiful out of pain.

And as my fingers learned new patterns, my heart started to release things I didn't even know I was holding onto.

Fear.
Guilt.
The need to be understood without having to explain myself.

Sometimes I'd play in the early morning, when the sky was still pink and the rest of the world was asleep.

Other times, late at night, sitting by the fire pit, cigarette in one hand, pick in the other.

The Boy Named Boy

I never needed an audience.

I just needed truth.

And music has always been the most honest thing I've ever known.

A few years ago, a friend of mine—Col. Perry Sullivan—reached out.

Retired Air Force, sharp as ever. He was working on a book about his father, a legend in North Carolina named Percy Flowers. The man had been a moonshine runner, a foxhound hunter, a larger-than-life figure with stories so wild you'd think they were fiction.

The book was called Lost Flowers.

Perry wanted to bring it to life—not just with words, but with music.

And he asked me to write it.

Ten songs.

Music in My Blood

That was the goal.

I wasn't sure if I could do it—at least
not fast. But once I started, the songs poured
out like they'd been waiting their whole lives to
be written.

I wrote the entire album in five days.

Lyrics. Melody. Guitar parts. The
rhythm. The soul of it.

It all came together like I was being
handed something from somewhere else. Like
the story didn't just belong to Percy—it
belonged to all of us who've tried to survive the
weight of a complicated legacy.

The songs were about more than just
bootlegging and hunting dogs.

They were about fathers and sons.

About freedom and memory.

The Boy Named Boy

About the lines between legend and
truth.

And writing them helped me understand
something I hadn't been able to put into words
about my own life:

Sometimes we carry the story of
someone else so we can finally hear our own.

Perry loved the songs.

They're being produced now in
Georgia, put to music the way I imagined them.
There's talk of live performances, maybe even
a soundtrack release.

But honestly?

The real reward was just writing them.

Because every verse, every chorus,
reminded me that I wasn't just a veteran...

I wasn't just a man with a past...

Music in My Blood

I was a storyteller.

A survivor.

A voice.

I still play.

Not every day. Not always for long. But the guitar is never far from me.

It leans in the corner of my room. Rests beside the porch chair. Waits near the fire pit like an old friend who knows I'll come back when I'm ready.

And when I do—when I pick it up and let my fingers move—I remember who I am.

These days, I mostly play for myself.

Sometimes Patricia will sit and listen. Sometimes Ziarah will walk by and smile without saying anything. Sometimes one of the older kids or grandkids will ask, "You write that one?" and I'll just nod.

The Boy Named Boy

Because most of the time, I have.

And I'm still writing.

New songs come in flashes. Sometimes in the middle of the night, sometimes while working on the farm. I keep a notebook near my bed, scraps of lyrics jotted on feed receipts or envelopes from the mail.

I'm also rerecording the older ones— tightening the sound, finding new edges in familiar lines.

There's something powerful about going back to your own words and realizing they still hold up. That the man who wrote them is still in there, still singing.

Music never let me down.

It never lied to me. Never asked me to be someone else.

It just waited.

Music in My Blood

It waited through the fights, the
silences, the moves, the deployments, the years
when I couldn't find the right words.

It was there when Frances forgot me.

It was there when I found my birth
mother's name.

It was there when I walked through
fields, unsure of where my life was headed.

I used to think music was something I
did.

Now I know—it's something I am.

A rhythm passed down.

A truth carried forward.

A voice that never went silent, even
when I did.

Chapter Thirteen:
Reflections from the
Ridge

There are people I never got the chance to know.

Not because they didn't exist—but because they stayed just out of reach. Held back by time, fear, denial, or death.

My biological mother was one of them.

She gave birth to me and gave me away. And when I finally found her—decades later—she denied it.

Even with DNA. Even with the names. Even when everything lined up, she looked me in the face and said it wasn't true.

I wasn't looking for an apology.

I just wanted acknowledgment.

To be seen.

She never gave me that.

And now, she's gone.

There was also Joe's mother—a woman who knew my biological father, Larry Ewing, better than anyone. She could've filled in so many blanks. Could've told me what he was like as a brother, as a boy, as a man before the war hollowed him out.

Joe promised we'd talk. That his mom had things to share.

But before we got the chance, she died suddenly.

Another story gone before it could be told.

The Boy Named Boy

I think about Dolores and Alfredo, too.

We were once inseparable. Kids stitched together by circumstance and survival. We knew each other's secrets, habits, silences.

But somewhere along the way, they drifted.

And now? We barely speak.

There wasn't a fight. Just a slow fade. Missed calls. Unanswered texts. Holidays that came and went without a word.

It's not anger I feel.

It's grief for something that used to feel like home.

Sometimes, what hurts the most isn't who left.

It's who stayed silent when you needed to be remembered.

I never expected money.

Not from Frances. Not from Tino. Not after everything.

But I did expect the truth.

I was named power of attorney and executor of their estate. That's what they told me. That's what the paperwork said. I took that role seriously—not because I cared about the title, but because I thought, maybe this means they trusted me in the end.

Then Frances got sick.

Alzheimer's.

And somewhere in the haze of her decline, something shifted.

Turns out, while she was fading, my sister stepped in—and convinced her to change the will.

Took me out.

Took the house. The land. Over half a million dollars in assets and left me with nothing but a memory of who I thought they were.

She did it clean. Quiet. Legally.

I found out after the fact.

No phone call. No explanation. Just paperwork and silence.

The betrayal wasn't about the money.

It was about erasure.

I helped raise this family when it was breaking apart. I stood by Tino. I pulled Frances off Alfredo when she was violent. I stayed close when others drifted.

And now?

They rewrote the story like I'd never been part of it.

I'm in court now. Fighting it. Not because I'm bitter—but because I refuse to disappear.

Because there has to be a line somewhere where the past can't be redrawn by greed.

She was always clever, my sister. Always thinking two steps ahead. Always playing the long game. And I didn't see it coming—because part of me still believed we were on the same side.

But we weren't.

Not really.

And maybe we never were.

Even growing up, I should've seen it.

Dolores and Alfredo—both Mexican by blood—never learned a word of Spanish.

But I did.

The Boy Named Boy

I speak it fluently.

Funny how the kid who wasn't supposed to belong ended up understanding the culture more deeply than the ones born into it.

For every person who walked away, someone else showed up.

For every door slammed shut, another cracked open quietly, just wide enough for me to step through.

I didn't get the mother I deserved.

But I found cousins who see me—who call me family without hesitation. I found a sister whose face mirrors mine so closely it still stops me cold.

I didn't grow up in a house full of warmth.

But I have a home now—sixty acres of land, a place I built with my own hands, surrounded by trees and time and peace.

I didn't always feel like a father.

But I've raised children who are strong and kind and capable.

Joshua, working in construction.

Cody, building warehouses.

Brandie, putting in work with Jonah.

Ziarah, still under my roof, growing up grounded.

And Axel, my youngest—running through the same fields I once walked alone.

I lost a court case.

But I kept my character.

I lost touch with siblings.

But I gained a family who came looking for me before I even knocked.

I didn't get answers to every question.

But I got clarity.

Not because anyone handed it to me, but because I stayed long enough to find it on my own.

I used to think legacy was about what people left behind for you.

Now I know—it's about what you leave standing after they try to erase you.

To anyone reading this who's ever felt forgotten—I see you.

To the adoptee who doesn't know where they come from...

To the veteran lying awake at 2 a.m. wondering if anyone would notice if they were gone...

Reflections from the Ridge

To the kid who learned to survive in silence because love came with conditions—

I've been you.

And I want you to know: you don't have to stay there.

It took me decades to learn this, but I'll say it plain:

You are not your paperwork.

You are not your trauma.

You are not their version of the story.

You are what you build.

You are the people who show up when it matters.

The notes you play when no one's listening.

The silence you turn into peace.

The Boy Named Boy

The scars you turn into songs.

People tried to forget me.

Even my own mother wouldn't speak my name.

But here I am—on my own land, with my own family, telling my own truth.

They listed me as "Boy" on my birth certificate.

But I gave myself a name.

And I lived it into something real.

Epilogue:
The Boy Named "Boy"

Some stories don't end.

They settle.

Like dust after a long storm. Like water returning to stillness after the boat's gone by.

Mine isn't tied up with a bow. There are still questions I'll never have answers to. People I may never speak to again. Wounds that don't bleed anymore, but still ache when the weather changes.

But I'm here.

Still waking up before the sun.

Still feeding animals.

Still writing songs that sound like truth.

The Boy Named Boy

Every now and then, I think about the beginning.

The hospital.

The certificate that didn't list a name—just "Boy."

The charity. The paperwork. The ride home to a family that didn't understand what they were taking on.

And then I think about today.

My wife, Patricia.

My kids.

My grandson.

My trees.

My songs.

The peace didn't come fast.

It didn't come easy.

The Boy Named "Boy"

But it came.

Because I kept showing up. For myself. For the people who matter.

I'm not looking to be remembered by everyone.

Just by the ones who know what it means to keep going.

And if someone finds this story one day—some young man looking for his name, his place, his people—I hope he knows:

You can come from nothing and still grow into someone.

You can be forgotten and still make yourself unforgettable.

You can be just "Boy"...

And still become a man worth writing about.

The Boy Named Boy

The Boy Named "Boy"